BENT SPOKES
AND
BROKEN DREAMS
COLLECTED SCRIBBLINGS
(AND THEIR CONNECTED SIBLINGS)

Don "Bent Spoke" MacKellar

Wider Perspectives Publishing ¤ 2022 ¤ Hampton Roads, Va.

"Outside of a dog, a book is man's best friend.
Inside of a dog, it's too dark to read!"

Groucho Marx

The Illusion Of Free Will

Echoes of the early 21st Century
as they were heard by Me

Some of these thoughts are archival
Most of this book is not
The paper is water soluble
The binding subject to rot

Some were composed while riding
Some while lying in bed
Each of them plucked out as they were
from the depths of my well-scrambled head

BENT SPOKES
AND
BROKEN DREAMS
COLLECTED SCRIBBLINGS
(AND THEIR CONNECTED SIBLINGS)

I've been writing and performing at spoken word events
under the Pen Name "Bent Spoke", not because I twist my
words, but because I've been a bit hard on the wheels of
my motorcycles from time to time, most recently while
riding home from the 35th Street Venue in Norfolk,
Virginia on the 8th of August 2016 when some kid texting
in a borrowed SUV drove straight into the back of my
motorcycle
(and me).
That not only bent the Spokes, it bent the Frame
I've been living up to that "Bent Spoke" Name!

> I often sing myself a song
> as I'm riding merrily along
> pistons pounding out the beat
> that I can feel right through the seat
>
> But I usually forget the correct lyrics
> of the songs that get stuck in my head
> so I "Fake It", make up new words
> and end up with
> "Original Compositions" Instead!

Editing Assistance by Faith Griffin

1st run released October 2022, Hampton Roads, Virginia
copyright ©2022   Donald B. MacKellar, writing as Bent Spoke
ISBN: 978-1-952773-65-5

Contents
(Or Discontents, as the case may be)

A Twist of the Tongue

Simple Addiction and Subtraction
Word Games
A Questionable Practice
A Web of Words
"Realing and Writhing"
Nature Abhors a Vacuum
An Ekphrastic Poem
Look It Up
Stringing You Along

Simple Addiction and Subtraction

The goal was to add verse to verse,
　but so far these few lines
seem to have gone from bad to worse,
and the final result is quite adverse
I'd been looking forward to perfection,
　but it looks like the reverse
now I wish these words I've gathered
　would just quietly disperse

Word Games

In the beginning was the word
or so I'm told, and so I've heard

Would there be things
without words to name them?

Could there be thoughts
without words to frame them?

Is there some kind of difference in between
what I think I see and what is seen?

or perhaps a difference between what is seen
and what I imagine there might have been?

> Am I part of It?
> Is it part of me?

> Am I a part of all I see?
> Or is It all apart from me?

I have my own particular point of view
and you have your frame of reference, too

When we talk about what we feel
Do the words ring true and make it real?

Or is all our talk just noise and confusion?
Does everything we say describe an illusion?

It Looks to me like there's no way to Tell,
but I'll continue to look and talk as well!

A Questionable Practice

If I declare that the stuff I write is Poetry,
does that make it such?
or does hinting that I'm not quite sure
mean I've already asked too much?

Will it destroy my credibility
if I question my ability?
Was there any credibility to begin with?
Is my poetry just a myth?

not sure if I care what others say
and I'll just keep writing anyway
I'm only writing because I find
once out on paper also out of mind

After I've written what I have to say
I won't have to think it anymore today

*My friend Richard read my remarks and wrote: "Couple
of things. W.H. Auden once said that like a motorcycle, a
poem should work. At least that's how I remember what
he said. Another thing: Even Chaucer wouldn't have
called himself a poet and he practically began the show
for us. The word then was "maker," so I've always
considered myself a maker. "Poet" is what other
people may call you long after it doesn't matter
to you any more"*

A Web of Words

Words help to say
what we are trying to think
and can also be written
         with paper and ink

I weave a web of words,
yet my thoughts
slip through the holes
in my sentences

A line of words strung together
is sometimes not enough of a tether
to tie up the thoughts we attempt to convey
so no one understands what we are trying to say

You may understand what
each word may mean,
but the message of the sentence
escapes in between

If words aren't matched up precisely
the thought they are meant to convey
may slip away between the words
         and listeners won't understand

What we are trying to say
so be careful about the way
you line up each word so folks
will understand what they've heard

"Realing and Writhing"
(Spelled "R-E-A-L-I-N-G")

With apologies to Lewis G. Carol's Mock Turtle,
who spoke of "Reeling and Writhing",
when he meant "Reading and Writing"

When you read what I write
you can see what I say,
but I'd Like to speak
directly to you today

And when I speak to you Here and now you will
have to listen to Hear what I say because there is
a huge difference between what I've written on
the page and what I say to you up on the stage

Written words and spoken words are very
different things: You might say written words
are dipped from ink wells while spoken words
flow from artisanal springs

All poets have a thirst for knowledge
in either case the artist slakes our thirst,
and neither is either better or worst
written words and spoken words

are just . . .   Different
When I wrote those words upon the page
I had to put three dots between the words,
an ellipsis, to show there was a pause, but when
I spoke   I just . . . held back a second

6

and I could do that because . . .
written words and spoken words are just
                    . . . Different

Audience is the correct term for you recipients
                of the spoken word
Audio = transmission or replication of sound:
I don't know what you call a group of silent readers,
I confess: Critics, mostly I would guess

If a reader doesn't understand what the writer said,
a reader can re-read the entire paragraph, but if a
listener didn't hear or understand what was said
the speaker has written their own epitaph

It took me a while to see that, but now that I have heard
(a mixed metaphor ?) I have to think about
how I'm going to use each word

Is my word intended to be read, or shall I speak it
back to you instead? After my written work has
been composed I know exactly what is in it,
but I would have to speak it back to you
at a rate of 15 lines per minute

Not only are they different, so is their skill set:
once you have written out your words for reading,
what you see is what you get

Spoken words and written words aren't
quite the same even when they are the same word
because the way it looks upon the page may sound
                completely different on the stage

Some venues (hint, hint) are very performance oriented,
where the words of the poets are not politely read upon the
stage:
No indeed, "Their words leap right off of the page
                and write into your face!"

Now there's an intentional example of a written pun
that doesn't work as a spoken word:

I wrote "Their words leap RIGHT off of the page",
spelled R-I-G-H-T, but the second half of the sentence
"write into your face" is written and spelled W-R-I-T-E:
and not "Their words leap right off of the page and right
into your face !"

Written words and spoken words are both
delivered from the heart, but the methods of
delivery are two entirely different forms of art.

You have been listening to where I'm trying to go,
but I'm obviously not there yet, and until the day
I can learn what I've written by rote,
what you see is what you get:

Just me struggling to read
whatever I've written on the page
"Bent Spoke" indeed!
twisting, realing & writhing
here upon on the stage.

Nature Abhors a Vacuum

I don't like leaving this page blank,
so I just continued to type in the hope
a flow of words will somehow populate
this empty Space

in a manner that will grace the page
to leave a more balanced look that more
closely resembles a well thought out book,
and not just an attempt
to change that empty look

and I've made some progress along
those lines by typing a few
and spacing stanzas
to make this look like a
masterful composition

when all I'm really trying to do
is populate this space
to fill the page more completely,
so it doesn't look quite so
empty and forlorn

I think it looks better already
How about you?

An Ekphrastic Poem Inspired
by the Poem "*Ode on a Grecian Urn*"

I don't owe anything on my Grecian urn
I paid cash for the darned thing

Probably paid as much as the average
Greek earns during an average week

because the Greek economy is a disaster,
been that way for many a year,

I'd call it an impending disaster
if it wasn't already here

"Ode on a Grecian Urn" is a poem
written by the English Romantic poet
John Keats in May 1819 and published
anonymously in January 1820.

"Look It Up"

No, I don't want to bother
looking that one up

I never attended prep school,
before I was an undergrad,
but after I became one,
I met several lads who had

One of my favorite stories that Keven
told to me, concerned a word an
Andover Prep classmate had invented
with a peculiarity

The word was "insegrevious"
and he challenged his classmates to see
if they could slip it into written assignments,
since it looked quite scholarly,

but of course, it wasn't listed
in any dictionary that you could find
and in fact the word had even been
left intentionally undefined

"We attempted to explore the relationship
between common factors in the set,
but our results were insegrevious,
and we have not defined it yet"

or

"The effect was insegreivous, and
no one was harmed by their efforts"
are both good examples of attempts
to fool professors into allowing use
of the word to slide right on by,

This was long before "spell check"
would highlight the word
and back in the daze those prep school
boys were certainly very sly,

but of course, they never meant harm to
anyone and, by now, it's plain to see
those episodes were just a light-hearted
prank committed insegreviously.

Stringing You Along

Sometimes I wish I could write
the way words were combined
in strings of words I've read

and not in the collections of words
that I string up instead
Words that never work

as well on the page
as they seemed to in my head,
but then, of course

I write with my left hand
which doesn't work very well
for much of anything else either

Apparently talent is not a
universally scarce commodity
although it may have skipped me

My writing seems to suffer not only
from arthritis in my left hand, but also
from the equivalent of arthritis

in the joints of my head, but at least
I've managed to string you along this far
without even snapping the thread

In the Blink of an Eye

See Saw
Seeing Double
A Work in Progress
Super-Vision
Watch Your Language

See Saw

Our minds lack the mental agility
to interpret everything we are able to see

We label parts of the picture with words that fit
to filter out each thinkable bit

If the label doesn't fit what you are thinking about
your mind's eye will filter that image right out

We invent our own worlds as we see fit
as we filter experience, bit by bit

We look with our eyes, but we see with our mind
to interpret whatever our eyes can find

So, it's easy to see right off the bat
we never see all of what we're looking at

there is always a built-in flaw
to whatever you think that you saw

Seeing Double

We're both looking,
but the image that you see
may appear completely
different to me

Unless you focus carefully
you might also find
your image altered
            by your mind

Your eye is the lens,
but your mind is a filter
and sometimes the two
can get out of kilter

We may ask each other what we think
of all the things we see,
but everyone else's viewpoint differs
from the way those same things look to me

It's really quite a wonder
we agree on anything at all
since the very concept of "me & you"
separates "us" by a wall

So, take a look through my eyes
to see my point of view
and while we're at it
show me a peek through yours too

A Work In Progress

Why do you eat what you eat?
Why do you drink what you drink?

Why Do You Write What You Write?
Why do you think what you think?

You had to be carefully taught
whatever you think that you thought

You had to learn what to do
to believe you are actually you

Apply a label to "things" that you see
to filter out the confusion

Line up every "thing" linearly
to help complete the illusion

We invent our own worlds as we see fit
as we filter experience, bit by bit ·

That's how you became you
That's how I became me

That's the way we become we
You have to be taught what to see

Super-Vision

The "Things" that you see
don't actually exist
until you look right at them

Rainbows are only seen
by beings with color vision
who are looking at "rain" or "mist"
between themselves and the
source of "sunlight"

With rainbows it's relatively easy
to see right through the illusion,
but you must look a lot harder
to see that stuff like granite and people

are also just an optical occlusion

Watch Your Language

"Watch Your Language" we were
admonished, and I was astonished
that anyone could actually do that
without first writing it down

Otherwise, unless you "speak"
by signing with your hands and fingers
I don't see how you can
"Watch Your Language"

You can only watch your language
by reading your lips in a mirror,
but if you write down what you
are going to say, everyone can see it

Time and Space

Insightful Outlook
Just Like Yesterday
Entropy
A Tarot Card Tucked in With Ancient Maps
Thinking Ahead
Time Travel
Let There Be Light
Tic Toc

Insightful Outlook

I can still see the stars although
I've been told they're not exactly there
because they've moved someplace else
          (but I'm not sure where)

The light some emitted
still twinkles above
while others have collapsed into
the "stuff" we're made of

"Matter" is just a pattern of energy
that helps the light give "us" something to see
Our "mind's eye" provides a unique point of view,
and a frame of reference for everything else too

So far, an insightful outlook
is all my mind's eye can find,
but I'm not sure if "I" am inside
          or out of my mind

Just Like Yesterday

The other day I was overcome
by a sense of Déjà vu,
and I'm told we've all been here before,
but not as me and you

The stuff we're made from
is rearranged, over and over again,
the elements remain the same,
but the pattern is often changed

Your face looks different this time around
what once was sea is now solid ground
rest assured things will change again
the way a sunny day is erased by rain

Just like the last time, and the time before
Just like tomorrow, and forever more

If this all seems so familiar,
that should come as no surprise
It's all been here forever,
Is that so hard to realize?

We're focal points of matter,
a locus of energy
all you really have to do
is relax and let it be

Just like the last time, and the time before
Just like tomorrow, and forever more

If you wait a moment, It becomes a year
as your self-assurance is replaced by fear,
but like the night becomes the day
your sense of doubt soon fades away

Just like the last time, and the time before
Just like tomorrow, and forever more

Night and day, day and night
the sun keeps burning, oh so bright
'til it collapses down to less than a dot
and all that is, becomes all that's not

Just like the last time, and the time before
Just like tomorrow, and forever more

Entropy

There once was an order
more orderly than we observe now,
but every time we take a look,
it's more disorderly somehow

A Tarot Card Tucked in with Ancient Maps

in tribute to Serena Fusek's book
"Ancient Maps and a Tarot Pack":

Crows spend their days on my front lawn and
in the tree branches adjacent to the balcony,
their voices a deep dynamo hum that echoes the
"thrum of cosmic blues" tangled up in the string
theory of whatever universe they spring from.

the white cotton shirt from Nepal that I wore
in the kayak at Little River is stained with sunblock
but is still white enough for the ghost dance
that so far hasn't brought anyone back
from wherever death has taken them

when the street lamps come on here,
they outshine the stars, but this street is
so far from the Avenue, I can't really ever hope
to see her again in this neighborhood,

although I look past the lamps from
time to time anyway, but usually only find
the lady in the straw hat who walks her little dog
here in the evenings. They always nod at the crows,
who usually answer back.

Thinking Ahead

Although I lived to a ripe old age
all that's left of me now
are these words on the page

that you now hold in your hand
and there is nothing else left of me
since all those I knew

are now long dead, too, and there is
no other living memory of me
except these words as you can see

I was once a child
then had a child of my own
and he had children in turn

Lovers and partners known
at least for a while when we still
had lifetimes left to burn

Now those lives have been
left behind as will these words
when you have turned the page

Time Travel

Here we go again
one more cycle completely spun
another new orbit
around the same old sun

that orbit is not a circle, it's a spiral,
but it takes a bit of optic nerve
to see that any way you look
is an open ended curve

To see anything at all you have to bend the light
then everything that matters pops right into sight:
at least everything that matters at your particular scale,
and there's certainly plenty of difference
between a butterfly and a whale

What really matters is your point of view,
I've got my own, of course you have yours too
both tied in with our time and locked into this space
along with all the rest of the current human race
spinning on a planet, spiraling around a star,

It's so easy to forget that part of all we are
with so many daily distractions
and the intervening nights
a scenario of alternating horrors and delights

Go out at night away from the lights on Main
under a new moon and gaze up
at that brilliant band of stars we call the Milky Way
that marks the edge of our on spiral galaxy

Somewhere beyond the Milky Way, set against
a background of stars very much farther away,
under conditions that are just right, you should be able
to pick out an oval shaped smudge of light

That would be the Andromeda Galaxy,
estimated to contain over a trillion stars,
the most distant objects visible to the naked eye

There are only a few billion Human beings
sharing the planet with us, very much closer by,
yet some chose to remain distant

The light of the stars in the Andromeda Galaxy
has traveled a distance of over two million light years
and you are looking back in time, because by the
time star light reaches your face, the stars have
moved to some other place, and may have perhaps
become something other too

Each of the elements in the periodic table
was forged in the heart of a collapsing star,
or some more powerful cosmic event

We and our planet are made of star dust,
so when you gaze into space and focus on a star,
you are looking back in time at the reflection
of what we are, but whenever we try to look ahead,
we miss out on here and now instead

Life is a delicate blend of happiness and sorrow
balanced precariously between today and tomorrow,
and we are all time travelers

Thinking of tomorrow, reflecting on yesterday
wide awake or dreaming as we continue
on our way, a beginning we can't remember,
an end we'll never see, we're traveling together
on a journey, at least temporarily

Records of events stored mere neurons apart
in my cranial computer represent
experiences scattered across decades of time
and hundreds of thousands of miles traveled

and some may have become a bit unraveled,
so I'm not sure how many I can trust
or exactly what will become of them
when I turn back to dust

Perhaps we're just a pattern that has become
partially aware of what's going on around us
and I'm not even quite sure yet if there
even is a boundary between here and there

because all art, helps to erase the boundaries
that sometimes seem to keep us all apart
from the All of everything

Or at least allow us to step back
for a moment to realize that the boundaries
that we think we see may not be as real
as we think they are and that everything else
just may be that way too!

Then again, I do have a recurrent history
of severe head trauma, have been knocked
unconscious at least three times as nearly as
I can recall, have sustained occipital and parietal
skull fractures in at least three places,

and perhaps just spent too much time back before
the turn of the century during the late 60's
experiencing better living though
the magic of chemistry

Experimenting with LSD, mescaline, psilocybin, and
peyote, has a tendency to affect the way things look to you
and that may have altered my point of view

I think it's safe to say, the jury is still out on that
question, wrestling with their own collective decision,
so let's just leave it at that, let bygones be bygones,
and like Forest Gump once said,
"That is all I have got to say, about that!"

"Let There be Light"

And there was light, either provided by a "big bang"
or a divine spark from the fingers of a creator
who created us in his (and her?) image.

Since there are two genders, we as products
of any creation may look different,
depending on the gender you were assigned
or any other gender you may have designed.

I've had a difficult time understanding
the scientific explanation of "light": Sometimes the
Photon,
(a unit used to measure some aspects of the phenomenon)
behaves like a particle and sometimes like a wave.

People are like that too: Sometimes we seem like
physical entities and at others we are more like
metaphysical beings (Is your mind inside or outside
of your head?) We are not either/or, we are both/and

As a wave phenomenon, we expand outward through
time and space, not merely in the linear fashion as a wave
is usually diagramed, but spherically in all directions at
once although you can only measure and graph a single
vector at any one time.

Waves have high and low points that define their
amplitude, with an average somewhere in between
which seems to match the highs and lows we experience
throughout the ups and downs of our lives.

The wavelength describes the frequency of that oscillation
between the highs and lows, and the person experiencing
those events is the particle aspect if life is in fact just
another example of light: The Lightness of Being

Luminosity, radiance, reflectance, refraction,
absorbance, photons, waves, candela, lumens, watts,
spectra, hidden under a bushel or scattered
throughout the cosmos, I've had a difficult time
understanding any explanation of "light".

Eye guess I'm not particularly bright,
but maybe someday I'll get it right.
Light is a heavy subject after all, about as
easy to see through as a black hole in the wall

At the center of distant galaxies are black holes
like broken jukeboxes, where the music of the
spheres goes in, on spinning vinyl discs,
but nothing ever comes back out

Like the quarter you just lost
in a broken juke box trying to
play your favorite song. Neither one
is there anymore: No quarter, no song

Just the black hole of a coin slot on a broken
jukebox that sucks your money in like
black holes at the center of distant galaxies
where all light is sucked in,

but nothing ever comes back out,
until the nothingness collapses down
into a spark of awareness that
begins the process all over again
to re-create the Lightness of Being

Tic Toc

Just a key at the bottom
of the top drawer beneath
the kitchen counter
The drawer in the corner
that you use for all of the things
you no longer use

The key to a door or lock
guarding something of value
perhaps the key to your heart

That could unlock secrets
that kept us together
before we drifted apart

Now there's nothing left to unlock
just a key in the kitchen drawer
beneath a ticking clock

Seasonal Salutations

The Difference Between Lightning and Thunder
Howling at the Moon
Looking Forward to Indian Summer
No More Silent Footsteps
Slipping Through the Seasons
The Autumnal Equinox Has Passed Us Once Again
The Mirror of Your Memory
Multiple Choice Test

The Difference Between Lightning & Thunder

The flash is always separated from the bang
with a difference dependent on the distance
between where you stand or sit
and where the lightning chose to hit

Hopefully not close enough to hit you
with enough of a separation between the two
so you can count the seconds in between
the flash and the crash to determine

how far away the lightning struck
because the light travels
much faster than the sound
and hopefully you will still be around

To count those seconds in between
what you hear and what is seen
you will survive, and it won't strike you
if there's enough difference between the two

That critical difference between
lightning and thunder

Howling at the Moon

You only get to howl at the moon
for a finite and limited number of times
that's your "magic number" because
you won't know what it is

until it comes up
and no one knows
what magic
comes after that

So, pay close attention to
the march of the seasons
that matches the steps of our lives
and take time to howl at each full moon

from the Wolf moon of January
to the Snow moon of February,
even if there is no snow
at your feet from where you howl

Rest assured the Worm moon of March
will arrive on schedule as the earth is
turned over by them to prepare it for
the Phlox blossoms of the Pink moon

with April showers to bring forth flowers
under the Flower moon of May when Winter
gives way to put a Spring in your step
as you howl next to your moon shadow

Along the way to the Strawberry moon of June
and the Buck moon of July, separated like all the
other full moon risings by a dark of the moon,
when there are no moon shadows,

but the progression will continue with the
Sturgeon moon of August as the seasons
pass you by, punctuated by your howling
                as you track their passage

by the waxing and waning of the moon overhead
with the Harvest moon of September
marking the end of Fall when falling leaves
crunch under foot beneath the Hunter's moon

as the beavers repair their lodges for winter during
the waxing Beaver moon of November named after
their preparations for the Cold moon of December

The twelfth and last lunar cycle that marks the
end of another year measured by the daily passage
of the sun, punctuated by your monthly howling
at the lunar circle

that shines as it rises, lit by a favorable position in
relation to the sun regardless of whether or not the
sky above you remains clear enough to marvel
at the disc overhead

Howling is enough to demonstrate your
appreciation for the completion of another
lunar cycle to mark your temporary place
in the cycle of your life, so don't forget to howl at
the next full moon.   (You'll feel better for it)

Looking Forward to Indian Summer

The summer always flies by fast
this summer is now fading into our past
I did my best to do a few things
during the milder weather that summer brings

That weather doesn't seem mild when
temperatures top one hundred degrees,
but soon we'll be complaining about
how much we dislike the freeze

But for now I'm looking forward to Indian summer
and milder weather that follows that first frost
I'm trying to Spend each day wisely
and disregard the Cost

Of whatever I choose to do
in these last few days before fall
I can Hear Indian Summer whispering in
the breeze and am ready to heed the call

No More Silent Footsteps

The green leaves of summer
have turned yellow, red and brown
today they are like a snowfall
as they all float gently down

they cover up the green grass
they cover up the street
there are no more silent footsteps
as they crunch beneath my feet

Slipping Through the Seasons

The summer monsoon will be over soon
the Sturgeon moon of August has already passed
and the full Harvest moon is not that far away

There won't be any more thunder in the mountains
or rain every afternoon with raindrops on rooftops
                    beating out a summer tune

Nights are already cooler as are the morning hours,
petals have already fallen away
from fading Summer flowers

It's just the march of the seasons, that matches
the steps of our lives as we spring forth into summer
then slip slowly into a fall followed by a winter
                    none of us survives

So, enjoy the days of summer,
rejoice in the summer monsoon
fall and winter are on their way

                    Harvest time is coming
                    so make the most of every day

The Autumnal Equinox Has
Passed Us Once Again

Summer is over and fall is here
as shorter, cooler days are drawing near
with corn stalks outlined against the sky
their husks and leaves sun-bleached and dry,

but the leaves of morning glories
are still bright green
and in the morning sunlight
purple blossoms light up the scene

their flowering vines cling
to each stalk
along the edge of the field
and morning's glory is revealed

as sunlight shines on
orange pumpkin skins
that soon will be carved
into jack-o-lantern grins

At first I missed the passing of summer,
and I had a lot of reasons,
but by now I've changed my mind
along with the changing seasons

after all it's another
glorious day in early fall
and I guess I don't miss summer
so much after all

The Mirror of Your Memory

Objects in your memory mirror
may be closer than they appear
as visions of events long past or now far away
may be recalled as if they happened yesterday

at least until your spark of life winks out,
but that's not what this poem is about
it's about the way you yourself may
still be remembered after that day

so, hold your memories close to your heart
where they best close the distance of being apart
share your memories with others too
and in that manner, they will remember you

as a reflection in their mind's eye,
a mirror of memories from times gone by
Sometimes the memory mirror cracks or breaks
senile dementia or Alzheimer's is all it takes

to cloud the memories of what came before
and lose track of what remains in store
so that only others may recall
who those affected were before their fall

they have moved into another dimension,
& we're all headed for one beyond so pay close attention
to what's happening up ahead,
but keep track of what's going on in the rear-view mirror

work to keep your memory mirror clean
to reflect on what can still be seen,
                    both ahead and behind

Multiple Choice Test

Indicate the correct answer to each question by completely filling the circle beneath the corresponding letter on the Answer Sheet with a number two pencil.

Do not make any marks in the Test Booklet.

Fill in your Name at the top of the Answer Sheet.

Start by answering all the Questions you can and skip the difficult questions until you have completed the easy ones.

You will receive one point for each correct answer and have one point deducted for each incorrect answer and one half-point deducted for each unanswered question, so it is possible to end up with a score that is a Negative Number.

You will have ten minutes to complete the Test and you may begin now.

1. The correct answer to this Question is:
   a. True
   b. False
   c. None of the Above
   d. All of the Above
   e. Some of the Above
   f. The answer is true, but the question is false

2. Where are all the other Questions?

Musings (*Muse Sings*)

Dilemma
Tangency
What Do You Think?
Just Keep Typing
Bean Sprouts
Spiraling Around a Star
Random Thinking
That Second Cup

Dilemma

I've been blessed
and I've been cursed
but could never determine
which state was the worst

When trying to decide
between the two
sometimes the choice
is not up to you

I was awarded a simultaneous
blessing & curse
because I couldn't decide
which condition was worse

Tangency

If you take a straight line and bend it
you end up with a circle
If another straight line is positioned to just
kiss the outside edge of the circle
        at any point

the second line is considered to be tangent
to the circle and you have created tangency

I've rarely been part of the inner circle,
but I've been tangent to quite a few
and each of them certainly touched my life
as I was passing through

Never near the center
always at the outer edge
clearly not fraternity material
(I'd make a lousy pledge)

I seldom click and often clack
have rarely functioned
as part of the pack
because I've never really had that knack

Some folks always stick together
and form a faithful crew,
but I have rarely even stuck around
so those bonds just never grew

I've never quite
fit into the groove
so my record skips
and I've kept on the move

I have difficulty recognizing faces
and I can't remember names
so naturally I'm not particularly good
at playing social games

I've also got a bit of hearing loss
sometimes I can't hear what people say,
but I'm not anti or asocial
                even if it looks that way

so if you see me smiling at you
I hope you also See
although I may not be a part of your circle
I certainly appreciate our tangency

What Do You Think?

The meaning of life
has been earnestly sought
sometimes i wonder
if all for naught

There is even
a philosophy that taught
there may be no thinker
just the thought

What do you think?

Just Keep Typing

As long as what I write remains entertaining
hopefully I won't leave anyone complaining
about how they had expected better material
everything written is not ethereal

Most of what I write, is not very good
I'd write a whole lot better If I could,
but there's a fat chance of that,
as you can see and a much slimmer chance

I'll ever write real poetry,
so I'll just write about
what I see and the way all that
stuff looks to me

Some may say I wasted all the time that took
In reply I'll answer, at least I took a look,
but writing has become a habit
probably a bad one, too

You may not admit
that you have bad habits,
but I'll bet-cha
that you do

Bean Sprouts

Some folks bequeath a legacy
of all the things they've done
Others disappear without a trace
with nothing left but empty space

Bodies fade away, but minds endure
through music, film and literature
souvenirs of lives well led
gifts that persist long after we're dead

Following the faintest
footprints of dreams
to the ghosts
of carefully crafted schemes

Grainy images flicker on screens
depicting oft repeated scenes
that don't amount
to a hill of beans

Spiraling Around a Star

Happy words fading in bright sunlight
ink dries on words wrung
from the sorrow of night

Greeting the dawn as a daily surprise
grown a bit older, but not yet grown wise
still a singer of truth, and a teller of lies

Random Thinking

Is it possible we were designed to be free willed?
Can that faculty even be instilled?
Or is all our behavior automatic, autonomic,
anatomically auto-matonic?

Perhaps we are merely Animatronic
with a fiercely protected copyright
We are born completely helpless,
and all behaviors must be learned

At first you are fed, clothed and sheltered by others
who mold and shape you like them
with common goals and rules and roles
reinforced by rituals in the end

You not only have to be taught what to think
you have to be shown what to see
to actually learn to differentiate
between the concepts of "You" and "Me"

Awareness begins with the concept there is
something other than "Me" and we begin to think
that optical images and sensory inputs processed
in our Mind's Eye can actually be symbolized
by the single uppercase letter "I"

And that what is being processed is actually
being experienced by "Me"

Skin has the sense of tactile response
that can be felt as pleasure or pain
or cold and heat from fingertip to tender feet,
but does my skin feel like it separates me

from all the other "things"
or does it feel more like
it connects me to them?
See what confusion thinking brings?

The sense of sight suffers an even worse plight
it doesn't work at all at night but only when
there is enough of the correct wavelength of light
reflected and absorbed by every "thing" in sight

But do those "things" really exist
"out there" for you to see or were they
created only within the eye of your mind?
Where exactly can you find what you
think you are looking at?

You have pulled all those "things"
out of your mind like a magician pulls
a rabbit from a hat, except there is no
magician, no rabbit and no hat

Or at least sometimes
"I" have random thoughts
about the 'things" I see
that think out much like that

That Second Cup

Just finishing my
second cup of coffee
almost an hour
after noon

I'm still quite
easily distracted,
but fortunately

Only by things
that keep me
from finishing up

Everything Else
    I should
    be doing

Interstate Introspection

Kick Starting My Muse
Interstate Introspection
No Wars on My Watch
Intermountain Reverie
Spinout on the Highway
The Future Burning Brightly
Still Running
Behind a Cabin at the Riverside Inn
Rain on my Windshield
A Song of the Saddle

Kick-Starting My Muse

Sometimes my pen seems to glide
across the paper from side to side

Words penned up in my head
flow out onto the page instead

with very little help from me
some poems write themselves,
but things aren't like that today
I can't think up anything to say

Fortunately writing isn't all I do,
I ride around on Motorcycles too

So relief is a twist of the wrist away

Interstate Introspection

My motorcycle is a medicine wheel
that I have used to adjust the way I feel
any time I'm feeling down
I can start my engine and head out of town

There is always something new to see
as the road unwinds in front of me
that's why I'm going for a ride today
relief is a twist of the wrist away

The sudden rush of acceleration
focuses all of my concentration
firmly in the here and now of time and space
with a song in my heart and a smile on my face

If you don't enjoy your surroundings
you can leave them all behind
by heading out on the highway
to escape the daily grind

But as I've ridden across the country
from state to state I Find
contentment isn't tied to places or things
it's just a state of mind

My motorcycle is a medicine wheel
spinning just out of reach ahead of me
that never fails to take me to another place

nowhere near wherever it was I thought
I had to flee from, and before I realize
there was a transition, I'm headed towards
wherever it was I should have been to begin with

Here and now, time and place
adapting to the human race
developing a synchronous point of view
in phase with the way things look to you

still seeking insight for my outlook
still checking for a constant throughout the range,
but nothing stays the same forever
the only constant is constant change

Although I am still cruising the "The Interstate",
you know, that place you inhabit from the time you
realize you are seeking a path to enlightenment
until that new state is attained
and of course everyone's path is different:

For some a roadmap and GPS may assist
during the transitional period, or at least that's
what it looks like from here today,

but each moment breeds the next, and there is
no way I've found to get a peek at that until you
are already in it, when it's sometimes too late to see
you may have taken a wrong turn a few miles back:

Fortunately, there is still the next moment,
                    at least so far.
            content with my lot in life, today,
                which is temporary, just like
                        everything else

Motorcycles provide a sense of situational awareness
I'm very aware each day could be my last
so far my life seems to have flashed by very fast
probably because I spend a lot of time of it behind the
handlebars as my motorcycles flash by

Or sometimes get passed by other cars
and there have been times a ride
hasn't ended well when now and then
I've had to just sit a spell to heal up

Because I've wrecked a motorcycle or two
(the actual count is probably three),
but so far at least the wrecks
haven't quite killed me (yet),

but there have been times they almost did
during the crash at the end of the skid
when I recall waking up in hospital or ambulance
being told that I had been knocked out cold

because being unconscious
is exactly what it sounds like
I don't recall the impact at all

Sometimes I wonder if I'll wake up
at the Gates of Heaven or the gates of Hell
to be told my last ride
didn't end very well

But until then I'll continue on my way
thankful for each and every day
because I realize each day may be my last
and that I probably sometimes ride too fast
while tearing along the highway

Sometimes lately it almost seems
my life is mostly bent spokes and broken dreams
It's not like a well of deep despair
(Although from time to time I have been there)

And nowhere near what others have had to bear,
but I never seem to find time or energy to repair
holes in the fabric of my being
that I myself continue to tear

Sometimes the "Middle Path"
Is a dance between lanes of traffic
along the highway's broken white lines
that beckons from the next twist of the road

then disappears in your rear view mirrors
with just a twist of the wrist
Don't look back:
Pay attention to what's going on up ahead!

Perhaps some of the best advice I've heard or read,
don't look back too often of for too long while you
are enjoying the here and now, pay attention to
what's   going on up ahead

and always try to park your motorcycle in the
shade if you leave a black helmet on the seat of a
motorcycle parked in the sun,
it gets too hot to handle!

No Wars On My Watch

Although I was trained as a warrior
and served on active duty aboard
a U. S. Navy guided missile destroyer,
there were no wars on my watch

during that ten and one half year
period of my adult life, between Viet Nam
and Desert Storm, so I don't really consider
myself as an actual veteran of the armed forces

It was much more like serving in the Sea Scouts
and it often seemed as if our mission
during those Cold War years, was to simply
"Show the flag and frighten the fish",
as the saying goes

I was married for 20 years, when there were also
no wars on my watch, yet that marriage ended
in divorce, which opened the door to one of the
great loves of my life, at least for the six years
we shared together before she passed away

I'm not a quick study, and still am not exactly sure
what lessons, if any, I have taken away from each
of the events I have just described to you, or why
I continue to write of them as I do

Perhaps the effects of war still leave a mark even on
those who have been spared the fury of warfare
because of course the horrors of war continue to
lurk in the shadows of awareness
even within the innocent among us all

These days I consider myself as retired to a
base of operations from which I while away my
time as "second generation scooter trash", a pass-
time pioneered by my parents on their 1939
Indian Sport Scout motorcycle, and I too have
found solace in the song of the highways
and the call of the open road

Intermountain Reverie

Sometimes when riding motorcycles
in the mountains, the weather gets very cold

except of course when it gets too hot
and when the temperature is just right for riding
it usually rains

Spinout On The Highway

Some take the high road; some take the low,
depending on the way they are trying to go
Such are the paths we all must tread
right up to the end of the lives we've led

This time I think we should go all in
with a smiling face or a tired grin
as long as the bones still support our skin
let's take the earth for another spin

The Future Burning Brightly

Back when I started out on the road
the future burned brightly
somewhere up ahead

Sometimes these days it's more like a
dim reflection in my
rear view mirror instead,

but I'm still riding on that road
my journey not over yet
with paths still left to tread

and the future hasn't
even gotten here anyway
So I'm still looking forward to that day

The past has turned out well for me
so it's still quite easy to see
the future burning brightly
somewhere on the road ahead

Rain on my Windshield (As Usual)

Rain focuses your senses
and puts you here and now
there is no other where or when
just you and what and how

Sometimes what you get
is not what you would choose
what you make of it depends
upon the attitude you use

So you pick out the ending
pick one or both or more
and try to keep that thought in mind
next time it starts to pour

A cloud's silver lining
is not quite enough
to pay for wet feet
when times are tough

When all is said and
done you know
without the rain
there's no rain-bow

Maybe there is no pot of gold
at the end of the rainbow
sometimes just the end of the rain
is more than enough to wish for

I rode my 2020 Triumph T120 Bonneville motorcycle
4,247 miles to VA, MD, WV and back to attend the Little
River Poetry Fest in Floyd VA, the re-opening of the
Venue on 35th Street in Norfolk, VA and to visit my son,
daughter-in-law and grandkids during the first 15 days of
June 2021. This is:

A Song of the Saddle

Day after day on the highway
tucked behind the handlebars
lining up a way to pass the trucks
then passed by faster cars

Riding across the heartland
in sunshine and through rain
settled in the saddle
on the road again

Picking out the waypoints
for refueling and a drink
ticking off the miles in between
just thinking what I think

Trying to read the highway signs
and looking beyond them to see
the country unwinding with the road
and the way it looks to me

When the weather cooperates,
the ride goes very well
and whenever it turns nasty
the ride goes straight to hell

But the benefits outweigh the difficulties
and I guess I'd have to say
I certainly have enjoyed the ride
that I've been on today

Politics and Business

Equal Opportunity
Questions Difficult to Avoid
Alternative Facts
The War is Coming
Why We Invented War

Equal Opportunity

Chiseled right into
the court house wall
are the words
"Liberty and Justice for All"

and then they were all
released on bail,
another case of
liberty and justice for sale

Unless of course you
haven't got a buck
then, my friend
you are shit out of luck

about the way
your transgressions are scored
how much justice
can you afford?

Questions Difficult to Avoid

How do you put back together
anything so deeply divided?

How do you convince folks
who have already decided
on the way they are going to
look at anything regardless
of the way things look
to everyone else?

How can folks look at the same
set of facts and interpret them
in completely different ways?

How can we agree on what
absolutely has to be done,
before it becomes too late to do it?

I don't have any answers,
just questions asked
along the way,
but my list of questions
grows longer every day

Alternative Facts

We can have different opinions,
but we can't have different facts
 your opinions may be dead wrong
then again I may be mistaken

Only one of us is right
how can we resolve
our differences tonight?
We can't always disagree
and for our sake I hope that
someday you will agree with me

Because in this case at least
you have been misled,
your beliefs are mistaken
and you are dead wrong
there is no such thing
as "Alternative Facts"
Those are just outright Lies

Composed in Late August 2019

The War is Coming

The war has not visited this house (yet)
it only comes to us through the TV set

no it has not come here yet today,
but it affects us anyway

no sandbags line the garden path
no craters in the aftermath

of planes overhead that may be delayed
by weather patterns that have made

snow banks to show
where the sandbags will go

the war is coming
as we all know

Why We Invented War

There must be winners
and there must be losers
That's why we invented War

War is the only way to ensure that
everything is divided evenly
(And that we get a little bit more)

Death Takes Its Toll

This Space Available
Merely Mortal After All
A Terrible Toll
Another Note to Betty
Stone Cold Dead
Our Spark Not Yet Extinguished
Lessons Learned Over Time
Is and Ought to Be
Weighty Matters
Condemned
Burning Off the Haze

"This Space Available, Inquire within"
Seen written on the back of a toe tag
I once saw in the morgue
where I used to work

Merely Mortal After All

I've still got the will to survive,
but I'm beginning to doubt
we'll ever get out of this life alive

A Terrible Toll

Life takes its toll
and Death is the cost
Leaving nothing but memories
of those loved and lost

Another Note to Betty

Whiling away the day with your cats
They sit nearby and occasionally
stretch out a paw to lightly touch my leg
as I write this note to you

one has curled up on the couch
next to me and I feel his warmth
just as surely he feels the warmth
of my body flow back to him in return

I wonder how they felt
when they reached out to you
and felt your body slowly growing
colder beneath their paws

How long did it take them
To realize that you
would not be reaching back to
pet them or ever move again?

I wonder if they ever think about
you the way I do and I wonder
What I'll do when I reach out to them
and discover they have grown cold too

Lately I've spent a lot of time talking to your cats:
When you sit in my lap and I feel the warmth
of your being as you purr, it's almost as if
I could still feel her, here with us,
where she and I brought you as a kitten

The only difference is, she is gone,
and that empty place will always remain
a part of my life no matter how full
the rest of it may become

I guess that's another illustration of the term
"Bittersweet"

Once upon a time,
or for perhaps a time or two
my entire life was modeled as art
as interpreted by my point of view

every aspect of existence
was perfectly aligned
with the here and now of space and time
in the scenario of my mind

lovers and partners
amplified the illusion
simultaneously providing
clarity . . . and confusion

life together is wonderful
while riding the crest of the wave, but the
downhill run may not be as much fun if you
can't see beyond our short race to the grave

Sometimes we see qualities in each other
that bind us together as partner and lover
Living together is the art,
of balancing forces that drive us apart,

hopefully without ever breaking
each other's heart

Blue Forget-Me-Nots
awaken from amnesia
in the morning sun

Stone Cold Dead

There are no Stones to mark their passing,
the work of the Stone Cutters is
                    "Non-Essential"

No one was allowed to visit them
before they passed on
the risk of contagion was too great

Bodies stacked like cord wood
in refrigerator trucks behind the hospital
with no stone yet to mark their passing

News anchors broadcast the daily count not
from the studio but from their own homes
their books lined up on shelves behind them

For a 30 for 30 Challenge
this prompt from Day 26
(26 April 2020):   Stone

Our Spark Not Yet Extinguished

Sometimes life is like a dream
an intimate conversation or horrific scream
sometimes solo players
sometimes part of a team

members of an extended family
that helps maintain the gleam
in our eyes that look back on
times and places we have been

to wonder about the times
and places yet unseen
faces we have traveled with
some of which have passed away
to where no one I've known can say

and surly there will come a day
when our time too shall pass away
the spark or soul that gives us life
exchanged as if to pay
for everything that makes us what we are

a singular point of view
situated somewhere in between
an atom and a star
a spark of life that lights our way
from night to night and day to day

until the ultimate price is due
and death collects both me and you

Lessons Learned Over Time

All of the wonders we discovered together
have vanished into our past
which of course was expected

we both knew nothing is meant to last,
yet I never quite expected it
to disappear quite so fast,

but as least we recognized
the wonders we beheld along the way
even though none of them
still exist today

I remain here alone without you
still stuck where I am pinned
and even you, my love are
naught but ashes drifting on the wind

so I hope you others also plainly see
that everything is temporary,
especially you and me

Take care to appreciate
each and every day
because your days too are numbered
and soon shall pass away

Once the spark of life
has faded from your eye
all of your cherished memories
may become ashes drifting in the sky

Happy thoughts to everyone, until then
(You do realize that your thoughts die too?)
That's why I've left this record
of my thoughts here for you

Think of it as ephemeral,
a pause in the process of decay
just a rough approximation
of the way things look today

Think of it as a snap shot
that you took along the way
Someone else may discover again
on some long distant day

Think of it as a "Thank You"
for reaping what I've sown
as I walk along the path
I've come to call my own

Thanks to those who walked with me,
and then just walked away,
thank you for that pause
in the process of decay

Is and Ought to Be

It's plain to see what IS
Now it's time to consider what Ought
because by now it's also plain to see
that salvation cannot be bought

It's time our attention was turned
toward whatever remains to be learned
to determine which tasks we must undertake
if success on earth is to be earned

within whatever portion of our allotted time
remains as yet unburned

Now is the time to determine
the best use for each new day
and then live each one as fully as you can
before we all pass away

Each of us is assigned a limited set of days
That's your magic number because no one knows
when their number might come up
or what magic happens after it does

No one knows what happens after we die
Perhaps our human bodies are just a shell
and we are living within a chrysalis today
and not until after we die shall we awaken

transformed, sprout wings and fly away
or perhaps we'll just lay dead,
and not notice a thing
No one knows what gifts death may bring

Weighty Matters

The difference between
a head stone and a pillow
is a matter of considerable weight

My ashes shall likely
weigh less than either
once I have exceeded
my expiration date

Drifting lightly on the wind
perhaps scattered by a friend
regardless of how we live
that's how we all shall end

Unless, of course,
you are planted in the ground,
but I'd rather just have
my ashes scattered around

Dissipating on the breeze,
drifting lightly through the trees
with nothing left but the trace of a smudge
as the breeze moves on, but the trees don't budge

Condemned

Abandoned buildings are a lot
like dead human beings
the spark of life has left the body
and the soul has moved on

Both are just empty shells
the warmth of human contact is missing
you can't tell where it has gone
just by looking only that it is no longer there

The former resident and the abandoned residence
no longer share their ephemeral resonance

That is the difference between a house and a home
homes are filled with love and warmth and light
like the human beings within them
when occupants move on
only the empty shell remains

Same thing with the human beings
once the spark of love and warmth and light
has left the body, only the empty shell remains
if there is or was a soul, it has left the building

What happened to the former human occupants
of the abandoned buildings?
have they moved on to fill another vessel
to carry them to their next destination?
Were they alive or dead when they left?

Does that even make a difference?
After all, it's the spark or soul that
animated the human body
that actually moved on

"It" may have left both an empty house
and a lifeless human shell behind
What is the nature of the "it"
that did the moving?

Are we, the living, condemned to never
know the correct forwarding address
so that we can still keep in touch with the
late human beings, who have clearly
moved away,

> Even though they have left
> their empty shells behind,
> like abandoned buildings

Burning Off the Haze

As the Sun rose higher that morning
the clouds and mists on the mountain
burned off to a very light haze

Not yet clear enough to see all the way
through to tomorrow, but bright enough
to illuminate the corners of my memory

And evaporate the yesterdays
that lurked there in the shadows
where they sometimes

block the view of the path
that leads us towards where
we should be headed

and not back to where we were
before we learned to follow the sun
to where we are today

The sunlight filtering through the branches
from a viewpoint here below the tree line
is brightest along the correct path

to the summit of the journey
always onwards and upwards
in the clarity of the day

With only blue skies overhead
and no other Blues
on my mind along the Way

School Days

Our Study Group
School Mates
School Daze
Class Dismissed
We're Outta' Here

Our Study Group

Reviewing the entire course content
Together

facing the final examination
Separately

Planning on meeting at the student union
after that test has been completed

Hoping to see you there!

School Mates

This is not the only class we took
just one of a few we took together

Each with a different major concentration
both with a well rounded education

School Daze:
A Modern Triptych

An active shooter
has entered the school building
dial nine-one-one

You had better run
unless you decide to fight
or just hide in place

Someone lock the doors
stay away from the windows
duck under your desk

This is a modern day triptych,
just three short stanzas
each with three lines apiece
written in that 5-7-5 beat
we often associate with Haiku,
which this is decidedly not

It's just a modern day triptych
about School Daze

Class Dismissed

Wondering if what we discussed in the
classroom can actually be applied anywhere
as notes carefully composed in ink
now rattle around in thoughts I think

Everything dissected in the lab
was reassembled in the studio
now the class is over and it's time to go
on to whatever is lined up next

enriched by the total experience
and not just what was explained in the text
because the sum is always greater than the parts
and that's true for the sciences as well as the arts

We're Outta' Here

Climbing from the depths of disillusion
to a pinnacle of despair, what you might call
a stairway to heaven that never takes you there

Because of course Heaven doesn't actually exist
although there is a Hell, certainly a familiar locale
                    where we both used to dwell

In the Land of Disenchantment down along
the borderline between where we were
and where we are, it's been a long hard climb

and there is still a ways to go
so we'd just best get on with the show
Come on, We're Outta Here!

MON 11 NOV. 2019

Re-ligion

The Cost of Business
Bedrock of Faith
Creation Myths
The Value of Faith-Based Beliefs
Lucifer's Children
Quandary

The Cost of Business

Religions facilitate a transaction between God and man
Mankind promises to believe in and honor God
and God is expected to assist the believers
There is no "Money" involved in the transactions

But there seems to be a lot of "Money"
involved in the business of religions
Worshippers are encouraged to "Tithe"
or set aside 10% of their net worth for God

which sets up the priests or deacons as bankers
who then watch over the money
because God didn't have any "Interest"
in monetary transactions to begin with

One can only hope God watches over the
deacons and priests to help them work His will wisely,
but I wonder about God's skills as an auditor
because money wasn't part of the initial agreement

Money is just a cost of business tacked on by
the "middlemen" who intercede on your behalf
to help themselves
conduct the business of religion

The Bedrock of Faith

Fear and doubt are the basis for religion
we all fear whatever horrors our religious beliefs
        teach us to fear the most

Fear of an eternal damnation
tortured forever by the minions of the devil
and burning in hell for all eternity

Or rebirth into yet another life time
to be endured all over again, perhaps even
as some lower form of being

asif our current lives as human beings weren't
bad enough and although we sometimes doubt
that God or heaven and hell really exist

the fear that was instilled by our religious backgrounds
is far more powerful than the deep-seated doubt,
powerful enough to fill our prayers for deliverance

and to fill the confessionals and pews of the churches
the beliefs of others who came before us have built to
        honor their concept of a God who
        Must be Feared and Obeyed

Creation Myths

God as the Creator implies visions of some bearded dude
sitting on a throne decreeing that it should be, or one of
William Blake's illustrated poems with a naked, bearded,
elderly gentleman squatted on the floor with a chart and a
set of dividers to divide his creation into
      male and female, man and beast, good and evil.

But I prefer to think of a Creative Force that flows through
all things with no beginning and no end, or perhaps a
rhythmic, cosmic breathing in and out in cycles of creation
and destruction resonant with a more Eastern as opposed
to Abrahamic slant on things that side steps that whole
"Creator" trap, which calls into mind the question of
      "Who created the Creator?"

Because that question conjures up visions of the Earth
built on top of the back of a giant Turtle and we all know
how that mythical Native American version goes when the
True Believers begin asking, "What is the Turtle standing
on?"

"It's Turtles all the way down!", is hardly likely to
convince hardened Warriors that the Priests have
any idea at all about what they profess to know,
as compared to what the Warriors know about
conducting Warfare to defend that Faith.

The Value of Faith-Based Beliefs

Religions were invented before money
and both institutions are based on faith

Faith is the root of both the religious belief
that you may be reborn again after your death

and faith is the root of the belief that your money
will actually be worth something tomorrow

Lucifer's Children

Allow Me to introduce You to
the three daughters of the Devil,
there are the Twins,
Desire and Fulfillment

And let us not forget
their delightful younger sister,
her name is Regret
certainly one of the most captivating

Families I have ever met,
the Devil and his
lovely daughters
Desire, Fulfillment and Regret

Quandary

Allow me to ask you a question
that may seem a little odd
Did God create man?
or did man create God?

Short Stuff

Learning and Knowing
Keepers of the Faith
Random Four Line Notes
Good Morning
Focus on the Locus
Holding Your Future in Your Hand
Try to Be Joyful
Heads or Tails?
On Top of Buffalo Mountain

Learning and Knowing

The more I learn,
the more I realize
how little I know

Pause to read the word
ponder the correct meaning,
then go on from there

Keepers of the Faith

The accusers require no evidence
The inquisitors have no need for proof

All questions are phrased such that
any response is an admission of guilt

Each answer to the inquiries
digs their grave a little deeper

Random Four Line Notes

Libraries are
an attempt to ensure
the legacy of
our literature

With age I have found
much to my chagrin
my body grows thick
as my hair grows thin

I've discovered there is
still a bit of work required
even though I'm
now officially retired

Good Morning

Shrugging off
a sleepy yawn
eager faces
greet the dawn

Darkness fades and dawn begins
happy smiles and tired grins
here and there a frown or two
at thoughts of things we have to do

Focus on the Locus
and ignore the Hocus Pocus

Holding Your Future in Your Hand

I once had my palm read by a girl
who looked up at me and said,
my life line is so short
I might already be dead!

Try to Be Joyful

"Try to Be Joyful", a song by Ed Sanders
and Tuli Kupfergberg (who has passed away),
is still one of the best message's worth delivering.
Think Carpe Diem, not Crappy Diem
(Root Word: Re-Joy-Sing)

Heads or Tails?

Tragedy and Comedy are two sides
of the same coin:

The real question should be
not which side turns up,

but whether or not the coin
is genuine or counterfeit,

and even that is moot
if it is accepted by your creditors.

On Top of Buffalo Mountain

White mountains of cumulous clouds
tower overhead casting dark green shadows
across mountain ridges
rolling out of sight below

There are mirrors in your memory
heroes on the mountain
children on the pathway
climbing ever upward

Jack shouts through the wind,
"Almost lost my hat up here!"
There are worse places

Not Quite Haiku 4 U

Classical Haiku is thought and written in Japanese about a change that occurs in nature at a particular season with two thoughts set in juxtaposition with each other separated by a haiku "kireji" or cutting word. There are dictionaries of the seasonal notation words, and the short poems are written as what, in English, would be a five-seven-five beat or syllable count as three short lines, without punctuation or rhyme.
There are many schools of thought regarding other "rules", that separate haiku from senryu, which are poems about human nature, or Zappai, which shares that same three-line 5-7-5 beat, but not the seasonal notations, nor many of the other "rules" associated with haiku or senryu. I prefer the term "short poetry inspired by haiku", to side-step around all the rules, except for the 5-7-5 beat and three-line format.

Haiku speaks out in
many tongues in addition
to just Japanese

Almost Quadraphonic Winter Haiku

Snow falls on the ground
silence falling with the snow
blankets all the sound

Not yet quite frozen
the heart of a cherry tree
soaks up sweet sunlight

Broken by winter
the heart of the cherry tree
weeps tears that soon freeze

Frozen in its tracks
a deer watches as the truck
spins into a ditch

SENRYU (?): Not Winter Haiku

A seasonal note
that takes your mind someplace else
but it's not haiku

A seasonal note
separated by a word
that leads someplace else

Paper white as snow
ink black as the night sky has
frozen in my pen

Blank sheets of paper
and pens that will not be held
in anyone's hand

Not a cloud is seen
and yet a storm is forming
off in the distance

I have lost my pen
and thoughts I found in my mind
remain unwritten

Icy puddles form
glazing over the sound of
early spring peepers
                    (Not Basho's pond)

Butterfly on log
yellow wings spread open wide
greets the summer sun

Looks like another
conspiracy therapy
lots of that around

Pause to catch your breath
match heart rate to the mountain
breathing slower now

Stop to hear the sound
the mountain speaks like ravens
calling out to you

I already had
what I came up here to find
just out for a walk

Sometimes the magic
doesn't work the way it should
this is one of them

Non-Fictional Short Stories

I've written a few non-fictional "Short Stories".

Some of what I write about certainly never happened at all,
but all of my stories are true, of course,
because none of my tales are very tall,
they are "Short Stories", after all.

Added Almost as an Afterthought
The Luminous Lives of the Radium Girls
"Curiouser and Curiouser"
This is all about Nuclear Fission
Coal Men

Part of a Story I Once Heard
Added Almost as an Afterthought

There were numbers tattooed on her forearm
one of very few who managed to escape the ovens

at least that's what I was told by you about
an aunt in your family, a woman I never knew

from a generation that came before us
and I believe what you told me is true

in that offhand remark about your aunt,
a woman I never knew,

but the image remains in my mind to this day
although your aunt has long since passed away

The Luminous Lives of the Radium Girls

Radium, the radioactive element with an Atomic Number of 88 on the Periodic Table, was isolated and identified by Marie Skłodowska Curie with her husband Pierre in Paris, after she moved to France when the Universities in Warsaw would not allow a woman to study there for higher degrees.

The 20th of April is the anniversary of the isolation and identification of the radioactive element Radium by the husband and wife team of Pierre and Marie Curie in 1902. Since she was not allowed into the regular University in Warsaw Marie was trained at a clandestine "floating university" in Poland before following her elder sister to Paris for higher degrees. Her scientific work with her husband also included naming the first radioactive element isolated from Pitchblende ore Polonium, after her native country. The radiation eventually killed her: her fatal aplastic anemia is often associated with exposure to ionizing radiation.

Valued at 2.2 million dollars per gram, by 1917 Radium was the most valuable substance on Earth. Produced by the U.S. Radium Corporation, Radium was a key ingredient for use in luminous paints applied by girls, some as young as eleven with most hired in their teens, to coat the glowing numbers on the faces of clocks, watches and the dials of instruments that soon were in great demand during WWI.

They were called "The Shining Girls" when the radium paint on their skin and clothing made them glow too.

"Don't this stuff hurt us?" they asked as they were taught to dip their brushes into the Radium-laced paint, then put a fine point on the bristles by smoothing the tips between their lips, to kiss each dial they painted, as their concerns were also smoothed over. It usually took about five years for the aches in limbs and backs to develop as teeth wobbled, then fell out one by one (But the Girls continued to Glow, even in their coffins).

Years later Glen Seaborg, while working to purify Uranium and produce Plutonium for the Manhattan Project during WWII, was visited in a dream by the Ghostly Glowing Girls smiling through toothless gums, their broken bones still shining with the luminous radiance of Radium. That experience encouraged him to develop stringent radiation safety standards – still used today – to protect radiation workers from the hazardous effects of ionizing radiation. This legacy of the Shining Girls helped to protect me from radiation associated with nuclear power, nuclear weapons, and nuclear medicine throughout my own widely varied and luminous careers.

This is a true story I wrote in FEB 1982:
"Curiousor and Curiousor"

I met Karl serendipitously while we were riding on old Route 80 up in the Mountain Empire just East of San Diego back in February 1982. I was riding my spare parts special, registered as a 1937 Springfield Indian Chief motorcycle by the frame number. Karl's was an original condition 80 cubic inch 1937 ULH Flathead Harley Davidson. He motioned me to follow him to a "Biker Bar" in El Cajon.

Now Karl can spin yarns with the best of 'em, and what with various folks buyin' us beers and all, we spent a good couple hours just sittin' and spinnin'.
"Say Karl, how'd you get the scratch on your front fender?"

"Oh that's where I hit that mountain lion up in Pine Valley a couple months back; see, I scuffed up this right boot toe a bit in that one too."

"A mountain lion, Karl?"

Yeah, there I was just cruisin' along at about 60 when I noticed this light brown blur streakin' down the bank off to the right side of the roadway and then it's screech-squeal-slide-yowl and I'm sittin' in the road with the bike lyin', on its side a few yards ahead of me, engine still screamim', wheel's still spinnin', and this trickle of gas is spillin' down the road soakin' into my Levi's. The next thing I know, I've leaped up and cut the switch... Turned off the bike first and then checked for broken legs. It wasn't 'till after I got the bike on the side stand that I noticed this cougar layin' on the side of the road lookin' sort of dazed and confused an starin' back over his shoulder at me. Before I knew it I was over there jumpin' up an' down next to him yellin', "What's the matter with you? Don't you know what a motorcycle is? Look what you did to mine, you stupid son of a bitch, you could'a killed us you mangy good-for-nothin' crazy cat!", and it sorta' shook its head and dusted itself off and kind of wobbly-scrambled back up the road bank. He slipped and slid a little 'cause it's a pretty steep slope there, but he made it alright.

"Next time you're up in Pine Valley, look for the marks – a long black skid, some scrapes in the road, a dried up puddle of gas and a smear of blood with some tan fur ground into it. They were still visible a couple weeks ago when I went back through there."

Karl told me about a guy up near Live Oak Springs out in the mountain empire of southeastern San Diego County who has a bunch of old motorcycles up in his barn. I had the next day off too, so we oiled up our chains that Thursday afternoon and rode up to meet John and Alice Finn at their ranch near Live Oak Springs. John was sitting out on the front porch of the old ranch house, when we pulled in on our motorcycles and started swappin' stories.

Of course, John's a whole lot better at it than I am. I mentioned that I was in the Navy and John said, "Yup, I was in the Navy, too, as an Aviation Ordinance Man back in '27, got a battlefield commission during WWII and retired as a lieutenant in '56." As we wandered up to the barn to look at his old motorcycles, and there amongst the piles of old Packard and Model T parts, sat his 1930 BMW motorcycle.

"Yup, I picked that up in Shanghai when I was an Old China Hand back in '33. Alice and I rode it for years when I came back here to California. It's still got a Chinese I.D. plate on it."

I returned many times to look at their collections of antiques, guns and old motorcycles. After we left that first time Karl told me John was a Pearl Harbor Medal of Honor recipient. John showed me the citation one day, as presented by Admiral Chester Nimitz and signed by President Franklin D. Roosevelt.

"Always remember the 7th of December," was a mantra I remember learning as a kid and one week while watching Pearl Harbor documentaries on Pearl Harbor Day I caught an interview with John Finn, recorded when he was in his 90's. He was 32 on the 7th of December 1941, when he dragged a .50 caliber machine gun out into a field at the Kaneohe Naval Air Station where he could get a good shot at the attacking Japanese aircraft. The only problem with that position was the aircraft could get a good shot at him too. Hit 21 times by bullets and shrapnel, he continued firing for two hours and shot down at least one hostile airplane. John reported in that interview that hits to his elbow and thumb were the most painful, but that he couldn't even see the tiny pieces of shrapnel that caused those injuries, "But they hurt like Hell!"

One of the surviving Japanese Zero fighter plane pilots also interviewed almost spoke in Haiku of his viewpoint that day, too, in the manner of the Samurai warrior that he was:

"The bombers were like
dragonflies skimming the surface
of a very still pond"

The viewpoint of the 1,177 men lost on the USS ARIZONA was mostly filled with smoke and flames or flooded compartments and confusion. What had blasted their peaceful Sunday morning routine into death and destruction at the bottom of Pearl Harbor?
I used to visit John and Alice whenever I got a break from my shipboard routine. It was a nice ride up into the Mountain Empire; The wonder and junk-filled world of John and Alice. He told me that after they were married, they were only separated for 6 weeks during the remainder of his career, which included all of WWII. Alice passed away first in 1998, but John lived until 2010, when he finally passed away at the age of 100.

John and Alice are still one of the most inspirational couples I've ever met. Never would have met them if John and Karl and I hadn't all been interested in old motorcycles.

I got stupid back in 1986 and sold my Indian Motorcycle. All I have left to remind me of those years is this story and a few photographs: The first one is a copy of a Polaroid snapshot of me and Karl with our machines next to a couple of gas pumps in Descanso, CA back in 1983. Our faces are blurred, but you can tell who-is-who because Indians are Red, and Harleys are Black. Then there is John's official Medal of Honor photo with the medal on a ribbon around his neck, and a black and white snap shot of John and Alice on his black and white BMW taken in the late 30's just before the war. I always enjoyed visiting the ranch John shared with his wife Alice and her friends the horses in the Mountain Empire just east of San Diego near Live Oak Springs.

John said he never felt like a hero.

"The heroes was killed on the seventh of December 1941. All they got was dead!" is what John always said, so take care to howl at the next full moon, because we ain't dead, and always remember the seventh of December!

This is all about Nuclear Fission
(and Con-Fusion!)

In 1945 the United States government, anticipating invasion of Japan (and perhaps half a million casualties), ordered 500,000 purple heart medals that were actually issued all the way up through the Vietnam conflict. Prior to that requisition, over 10% of the annual production of electricity in the United States for several years had been consumed by the Manhattan Project to produce enriched Uranium and Plutonium for "Little Boy" and "Fat Man", the world's first two atomic bombs – the only atomic weapons ever given personal names or used to actually target a human population.

(At least so far)

The mushroom cloud rising from the ruins of Hiroshima could be seen from a distance of 100 miles. A few seconds after a nuclear explosion, thermal heat rays stream out from the detonation to raise the temperature of objects in their path to 1,000 degrees Fahrenheit or more. Wood is turned to black charcoal, and dirty concrete can be "bleached" by the thermal heat rays unless an object, such as a person, blocks the rays.

Human flesh and bones absorb the heat to keep it from bleaching the concrete and before the body turns to ash, it leaves an "atomic shadow" on the wall or on the street. Tuli Kupferberg and Ed Sanders wrote a song for their band, The FUGS called, "I Don't Want to Be a Shadow On the Wall". I don't either, how about you?

Russia still has over 7,500 tactical and strategic nuclear

and thermonuclear weapons, which makes the United States the number two runner up among nine nuclear powers with over 6,500 of our own nuclear warheads.

Myself, I was trained as a Nuclear Weapons Officer, Courier and Handling Team Supervisor at Nuclear Weapons Training Group Pacific, North Island Naval Air Station in Coronado, California back in 1982 because someone has to baby-sit the   damned things, which are fortunately slowly being destroyed a few at a time. We were taught not only tactics for how to attack with nuclear weapons, we were taught defensive postures as well.

The first indication of a nuclear detonation is a brilliant flash, brighter than the sun. (Can't be mistaken for anything else!)

We were taught at NUWEPSTRAGRUPAC, at the first perception of the flash, we should all immediately "Bend over and kiss your ass good bye!" That way you will at least die trying to accomplish something and you will leave an "atomic shadow" that looks as if you are "mooning" the bomb.

Those guys at NUWEPSTRAGRUPAC certainly had a sense of humor! I had a lot of good times there as part of what was simultaneously the best and worst job I ever had, and I was always anxious for the 45th President to "Make America Great Again"

I did my part by hanging out down by the Great Dismal Swamp on the border of Virginia and North Carolina just grating my teeth! That never made it any easier to swallow "alternative facts" or the undeniable fact that Donald John Trump had the ultimate weapons release authority for all the nuclear weapons in the arsenal of the United States of America!

Something I tried NOT to think about too often and I wish you all nothing but "Happy Thoughts" now that he is gone; may he rot in a privately owned prison cell with his fellow co-conspirators, and may God have mercy on the soul of any red, white and blue blooded American citizen who ever believed their pack of lies or cooperated with their joint criminal enterprise.

(Spoken as if there actually was a God who could intervene on your behalf and pardon or punish you for your individual behaviors but, of course, any reports of such Gods would be nothing more than "Fake News", so at least you don't have to worry about that!

Happy thoughts to everyone and "Ta-ta for now!" as Tigger used to say in those stories about Winnie the Pooh in the hundred acre wood.

I don't know why I'm laughing, none of that stuff was funny and unlike what our ex-President used to say to you, all the stories I just told you are true!)

Coal Men

The big Coal truck pulled up
in front of my grand-mother's house
and the driver got out to rig
the chute from the dump body
to the cellar window above the coal bin

As he revved the engine
to tip the dump body
coal rattled down the scuttle
mimicking the sound of Tommy guns
from gangster movies starring
James Cagney and Edward G. Robinson

My brother and I hurried to gather
small chunks of coal that fell from the chute
amidst the dust and clatter to fill
               our Little Red Wagon

We pulled the wagon around
to the back yard where Grand-mother
worked in the garden to proudly exclaim
"Look Grandma, we're Coal Men!"

Horrified at skins and clothes
coated in black coal dust
she hustled us off to the bathtub
after hosing us down with the garden hose
and tossing our clothes into the washing machine

It was a very short career as Coal Men

Odds and Ends

The Power of Positive Thinking
I'll be Leaving Here Today
A History Lesson
Life By Accident
Not Too Cool
My List of Things to Do
Reload Your Revolver
The Match Game
Sea Service: A Salty
Point of View
That Ship Has Sailed
Broken Heart Blues
Little Golden Moments
The Day of the Aftermath
An Early Easter Resurrection
Buoyancy & Stability
Lines
Edges Ledges & Hedges
Out of My Depth

The Power of Positive Thinking
(A Pretty Good Theme for Drinking!)

"You can accomplish anything you really want to"
but, of course, you really can't
My own thoughts have never really leaned that way,
but you're entitled to your own slant

Some see the glass half empty
to others it appears half full
I drink out of the bottle myself
would you like to have a pull?

It ain't empty 'till it's empty
and if it's anywhere near half full today
let's just pass it around while it lasts
and let the chips fall where they may

Temporary solutions
only work temporarily,
but everything is temporary
including you and me

Life is fleeting, so they say
so let's make the most of what we have today
there are many things we'll never know
now where on earth did that bottle go?

I'll Be Leaving Here Today

I'll be leaving here today I drank up the rent,
I guess you could say it just got Spent
I'm awful sorry that's the way things went
and my head sure as hell feels bent,
but it looks like I done drank up the rent

So I just stopped by to say,
that I'll be leaving here today
I'm pretty sure you don't want me around anymore
because this kind of thing has happened before
I'm awful sorry that's the way things went,
but it looks like I done drank up the rent

Thanks but, No, I don't Need a Drink Today
"Genius in a bottle, liquid courage on demand"
skeletons in the closet, the monkey on my back
                be damned
a hip flask in my pocket, a bottle in my hand
        no longer a part of my wardrobe
            a stranger in a stranger land
        walking, riding and driving sober,
                my eyes now cleared to see
            a brighter path in front of me,

        but that monkey is a trickster, so I must
            always remain aware that he could
                step back out of that closet and climb
                    back on, any time or anywhere
                        so thanks, but no
                    I don't need a drink today

A History Lesson

What passes as history
differs from what passes
as a record of history

we are taught a litany
of battles won that was
written by the victors

that which has been
vanquished is often obliterated
by the conquering warriors

assisted by priests eager to defend their
one true religion which will not tolerate
the beliefs, writings, idols, art or artifacts

of blasphemers, unholy ones,
and infidels whose works and ways
must be totally destroyed

although the ways of peaceful cultures
wiped out by the conquest were often
better attuned to and in accord with

the world that nurtured them than are
the ways of those who have mastered
only the art of warfare and who

write tales of victory that are
passed down to us as the basis
            of our history lessons

Life By Accident

I've become whatever it is I am by accident
with here and there a ding or a dent
as bits of change illustrating how
my life has been spent

in what sometimes feels like a
three ring circus under a big top tent
taken along and pitched wherever I went,
but I ain't broken yet (just badly bent)

Some folks maintain there is no such
thing as an accident, just "mishaps"
they say that happen when
everything is aligned that way

my mishaps occur regardless of the path I take
you can track my course by the ones in my wake
to mark wherever I happen to make a mistake
along a track I can see whenever I look back

In every case "mishaps" seem to line the path
I've tread so far during this life I've led
They've followed along wherever I went,
but I ain't broken yet (Just badly bent)

Not Too Cool

Again, I wish I was, and am slowly becoming
more literate and familiar with Poetry:

My closest brush with the world of Poetry occurred
back in 1968 while "On Leave of Absence"
from Drew University,

when I took a Greyhound Bus out to Cortland,
New York, where my brother Bruce attended
the State University.

One of Bruce's friends, James, was in charge
of scheduling entertainment and scholarly
lectures for the University,

which included an appearance by Allen Ginsburg,
who told me it "Probably wouldn't be Cool"
to accept the chunk of hashish I offered

him in the auditorium before his presentation,
so, I have it on very good authority
that I was "Not Cool" back in the 60's:

But Bruce, James, his girlfriend and I
got to have lunch in the Student Union
with Mr. Ginsburg after the show,

which was Very Cool, and James's girlfriend
gave me a ride to NYC in her brand new
Oldsmobile Toronado that night,

as I watched the peculiar cylindrical speedometer
roll up to an indicated velocity of 120 mph
along the way, which was also pretty cool.

I've had the great good fortune to be tangent
           to some very interesting circles
                "Interesting" being the word to use,
        when others might miss the mark or leave a bruise

My List of Things to Do

It's not as if I'm disorganized
I've got a list of things that I need to do,
but I may have misplaced it somewhere
around here and I thought about looking
for it yesterday, but I didn't have a clue

There are matters that require my attention,
and I was going to begin with the worst
so I studied the list for a little while,
but couldn't decide which to do first

My credit score is still pretty good because
at least I pay all of my bills when I should,
but probably never accomplish much more
than that (Although I certainly would if I could)

I thought about starting
another new list,
but the first one I wrote
really hasn't been missed

Reload Your Revolver*

Life is just a revolving door
You're helped in one side by your mother
We dance for a while between the two sides
until death helps us on out the other

Rest assured you'll come around again
to cry tears of joy and tears of pain
a different face, a different name
same old players, same old game

Don't ask why or even how,
but we're face to face, right here and now
you know I'd rather be skin to skin
so open your heart and let me in

You know we've both been here before
just like the last time and the time before
just like tomorrow, and forevermore
life is just a revolving door

(Of course, I don't believe that anymore)

* The lines above have nothing to do
         with the Second Amendment
         (Unless you have recently been shot to death)

The Match Game
or Reflections Regarding On-Line Dating

I went online looking for a match
it seemed like such a deal

The profiles sure looked promising,
but turned out more like flint & steel

Although the sparks were impressive
that's not what I was looking for

and now I'm not exactly sure
If I want to do this anymore

I'd still like to meet the perfect match,
but by now I should have learned

That playing around with matches
can get your fingers burned!

But what the Hell, I've got 10 of them,
and they don't even hurt much today

I think I'd like to meet you face to face
to see what you have to say

This is not the way we used to do this
back in my younger daze.

but I'm tired of the burning yearning
and not ready to settle for a smokey haze

So, I guess I'll keep on looking
for a partner to spend time with

although I'm beginning to suspect
they're just another urban myth

I'll just have to trust my Karma
to protect me from nasty stuff

because Evil also lurks online
I sure hope that my Karma's enough!

So much for "Security via Obscurity",
I guess I'm back online

your profile photo sure looks great,
and I sure hope that you like mine!

Although photos are only skin deep
they're what you see right off the bat,

but they only show the outside of your head
and there's a lot more to us than that

There are lots of lonely folks out there
judging by the size of the data base,

So here I am at my keyboard again
looking for a match to light up my life
                              Lost somewhere in cyber-space

Sea Service:
A Salty Point of View

After the ship had cleared the mooring
at the 32nd Street Naval Station in San Diego
as we pulled abreast of Coronado off our
port beam, while standing together on deck,
still at our sea and anchor detail station,

Senior Chief Bo'sun's Mate Henson gazed
longingly at a Carnival setting up shop onshore
and remarked, "Now there's a lifestyle I could
really enjoy … Breaking everything down
every few days and moving to a new destination!"

This, spoken by a sailor who had spent
20 years at sea visiting more ports and having
many more adventures than either you or me.

Before I signed on to see the sea my recruiter told
me, "The Navy is not just a job: It's an Adventure!"
although while stationed on the guided missile
destroyer USS BERKELEY (DDG 15), we used
to say, "The Navy is not just a job, it's a screw job!
… and this ship is a twin screw job!"

Adventures it would seem, tend to vary
depending on your point of view and
I'm thankful that my course in life has
left a few in the wake I've left behind.

Life itself is a carnival if you adapt
the right frame of mind and if you
don't like the course your life has taken
you can always change your mind.

That Ship Has Sailed

Sometimes I feel like the Captain of a ship at sea
until I realize there is no Ship, but only Me
Still trying to chart a course to keep my ship
from harm's way out on the briny deep

to pilot safely and not run aground as my
ship transports cargo half way around an imaginary
world that swirled and foamed only to be found
in my own head when I realize there is no ship,

that I'm lying in bed, and that part of my life
has just been dreamed and may not be as real
as it seemed because life is not always black
and white, sometimes it's gray

and not in living color like it is today
Sometimes the dreams are in color too and
there's no telling where they may take you,
like a blank sheet of paper and the restless pen

I find in my hand once again as I continue to
chart a course for that ship that does not exist
except when I find the image continues to persist
in my mind, although now I find myself

seated with pen in hand still dreaming of some
foreign land and wonder why as morning light
brightens the sky only to realize as I have grown,
there are many things that cannot be known

Broken Heart Blues

I went to see the doctor
when I was feelin' blue
and he told me my heart
had broken right in two

The doctor told me
there was no cure,
so I need a new one,
an' that's for sure

I need a new heart
this one's broken in two
I need a heart transplant
you broke mine clean thru

I'd sure like to get
that new heart from you
(and I could probably use
your liver too!)

While I was down I tried
to drink my blues away
and that's why I've got
no liver left today!

I need a new heart
this one's broken in two
I need a heart transplant
you broke mine clean thru

My heart's been broken,
and my liver's used up,
but a new heart an' liver'd
make me feel like a pup

So, I'm tellin' you
what I'd like you to do
just give me your heart
(and send your liver too!)

Folks think you're
heartless anyway
so send me your
heart and liver today!

I need a new heart
you broke mine in two
so just give me your heart
(and send your liver too!)

    No hard feelin's between us

Little Golden Moments

My train of thought is a lot like Tootle the Train
in those little golden books you may have read as a kid:
it very often jumps off the tracks, just like tootle did

Whenever Tootle got to that curve
where the meadow streams into view,
on his first few runs he would jump off the tracks
and my train of thought does too

and away we scamper across the grass
sniffing the daisies and dancing around
instead of finishing the milk run as we should,
distracted instead by all we have found

Tootle eventually returned to the tracks
and finished the task at hand,
but I'm still not exactly sure
just when or where I am going to land

I can't even see the tracks from here
and although I've thought about finishing
if I don't make a lot more effort very soon
my chances seem to be diminishing

I may never get where I was headed
whenever I started out,
but my thought process was never very rigorous,
and I still enjoy whatever I'm thinking about

and I don't work for the rail road anymore
my milk run days are over
it doesn't matter as much as it used to, now it's OK
for me to spend my time just rolling in the clover

The Day of the Aftermath

The day of the aftermath when
things didn't add up the way
you thought they might

When all the changes you anticipated
had slipped completely out of Sight and
the columns simply refused to support

the weight the additions have applied
and subtracting the remainder
doesn't work out either, even though I tried,

but there's no way to support the conclusions
based on the math involved and here on the day
of the aftermath, the problem could not be solved

If you can't find the solution in any other place
perhaps it's hiding in plain sight
right in front of your face

Despite whatever time it took
the solution is always found
in the last place you look

Breaking up is hard to do
Sometimes you have a breakdown too

An Early Easter Resurrection

It was a nice gate, but it was locked so I took
a walk down West Main Street, empty at this hour,
like many of the buildings on the odd numbered
side of the street this morning; Empty but well
maintained with fresh coats of pastel colored paint
and "For Lease" signs in the window

There was brick wall to my left now, taller than me
with a three-foot-tall wrought iron fence on top of it,
perhaps a product of the Tredegar Iron Works, half
 inch square vertical bars shaped like walking canes
with curved handles pointed towards the sidewalk,
painted a dark gray over several earlier coats of paint,
and I wondered

to myself if hydro-blasting or abrasive grit blasting
with walnut shell media, would be more effective to
prep the surface for the next coat: Either would be a
very expensive proposition, lead based paint removal
being as highly regulated as it is

turned the corner for a few steps to see what the wall
and fence were protecting – some institutional
looking middle of the 19th century brick building.
There are a lot of brick buildings in Richmond.
If they were stars, you could build a pretty
respectable looking Galaxy out of that many bricks

Walked past a coffee shop with two tables set out
on the street, a girl sitting alone with her book at one
and four septuagenarian men at the other, speaking in

cultured European accents. Thought about stopping for a
cup but walked on instead to a low brick wall about two
feet tall in front of a wooden building with a sign
proclaiming it to be some type of rehabilitation
center which seemed like a nice place to sit in the
sun, but Jack and Judith drove up just then, looking
for the Visual Arts Center, so I walked back that
way myself as they drove off in the direction I had
come from.

I meant to write about the two baby Possums
Jala Magik rescued from behind the 35th Street
Venue back in Norfolk that evening: Don't know
how I got off on a tangent about bricks and pastel-
colored wooden buildings on West Main Street in
Richmond, instead.
Delaney had thought it was a big cat nursing two
kittens, but it was a dead mama possum in the grass
under the big tree behind the Venue. Jala called the
Norfolk Police Department to get a hold of someone
from Animal Control on a late Saturday afternoon
the day before Easter Sunday. She put them in a
cardboard box on an old T shirt and they made
some high-pitched trilling sounds during the show.
The Possum Lady turned up after we had finished
discussing our presentation with the audience.

She knew exactly how to treat the tiny critters,
explaining they would be cared for with all the
other baby mammals, even though they were
marsupials, her rehab center apparently being non-
denominational. Who knew baby possums need to
grow until they measure nine inches from the tips of

their pointy noses to the base (not the tip!) of their
skinny, naked tails before they can be released back
into the Wild?

Written as #16 of a "30 for 30" poetry challenge
Easter Sunday 16 APR 2017

Took a course in the Navy titled:
Buoyancy and Stability

The Plim-sol mark on the hull of a ship
is put there so any observer

can gauge the state of buoyancy
to indicate how high or low the

ship is riding in the water
which is quite similar

to the function of a smile
on a human face

Lines
Thin lines, thick lines, long lines, slick lines

a thin red line holding the beach
a distant finish line just out of reach

the Long Gray Line marching at West Point
a line waiting at the door of the hippest new joint

a solid white line off to the right
a dashed white line stretching into the night

tearing along the dotted line
stuck for hours in a traffic jam line

a line that stretches around the block
workers in line behind the time clock

a circular line curving back on itself
a line of books up on a shelf

a line written with invisible ink
a line explaining exactly what I think

a line stretching all the way to the sun
a parallel line next to the other one

lines on the mirror, lines in your face
lines can be found just about anyplace

dashing off a quick line to a friend
eventually all lines come to an end

Edges, Ledges and Hedges

Edges are boundaries where
The end of one thing or event
begins again as some other thing or event

They may be limits
of something good
or the ending of something bad

Edges connect points or corners
as well as the planes or fields the surround

They are limiting factors that are allowed
to be crossed or may be designed
as limiting factors to surround and contain

Edginess is also expressed
as a feeling of
dis-ease or unrest

Edges always connect to
as much as
they divide from

To go beyond the edge
is to transition
to something different

than from where you came
even if both sides of the edge
are similar, or even the same

Difference itself is a product of an edge.
                        People speak of being
                              centered,

but it's the edges that provide the center,
the center is as far away as you can get
                         from the edge.

Edges may be linear, circular, spherical,
polyhedral or polygonal and are usually
combinations of several borderline conditions

Edges, ledges and hedges wedge together
                or drive apart, and an Edge is always
                        a good place to start

Edges are also a good place to end, my friend
                and the terminal edge of this page, I fear,
                    is drawing very, very near

In fact, you might say this edge stops right here.

Out of My Depth

genius in a bottle, liquid courage on demand
Ships on the Rocks have run aground
in some foreign land

Tiger Creatures Thunder, Juggler's Hands Bestow
as Crazy Prowling madmen Glisten down below

Dawn breaks into Autumn mist
condensing into Snow,

but there were no survivors,
no one will ever know
how that Voyage ended, all those years ago

although sometimes
when we're dreaming,
but not quite fast asleep

we'll catch a glimpse of timbers
beneath the briny deep

the story will remain untold
the mystery will not unfold

the secrets drowned men keep

Out of My Depth
*Inspired by a 64 word list distributed at
Poetry Readings by Serena Fusek and
Ann Shalaski at the Iris Art Center in
Poquoson, Va. and written as a Ten Minute
Challenge to use as many of the words as
we could to write a poem in ten minutes on
28 April 2018. Words here beginning with Upper
Case Letters were those selected from the list.
This is a transcript of my ten-minute composition.*

Slammed

What Did You Think About That?
Travel Lightly
Rounding the Final Turn

What Did You Think About That?

I'm not exactly sure about "The Way Things Were"
we all see events in a different way
and since our memory colors what we remember
who knows what we'll think back about today

Events we shared together
and all the sights that we could see
may not have been seen in quite the same light
and could be interpreted differently

Some of the times I thought were wonderful
others found completely horrendous
so there's never any certainty
regarding things that may offend us

The way you look at things today
may also have totally changed
so that over time your recollection, too
may be completely rearranged

It's even possible to have memories
of things that never happened at all
so I'm not too sure what I can trust
about anything I recall

Our experience molds us into what we are
based on what came before,
but memory is a such a slippery thing
I can't trust mine anymore

But there are times I think back on the way
        I felt in high school:
when I would look forward to "Someday"
"Someday" when I'll be older,
"Someday" when I'll have enough

Somehow "Someday" came and went,
now I'm elder with too much stuff!
I used to look forward to "Someday"
to do that now, I'd have to look back
"Someday" came and lasted quite a while
before my life took a different tack

Of course, I never saw that coming
and it happened a time or two,
but once everything is done (or undone)
there's nothing more you can do

Somehow "Someday" has slipped into Yesterday
and, although I still look forward to Tomorrow,
sometimes I look back on "Someday"
with just a touch of sorrow

Sorry that I didn't do more than I did
even though I appreciated what I had
most of the time I was happy,
but I know sometimes I made loved ones sad

Most of my time was spent sorting out stuff
that happens every day: it's easy to miss
"the way things were" even if they were
                    never quite that way

All too often I know my behavior
had a bad effect on those I loved most
I hope I've put those days behind me,
but some days I'm still haunted by that ghost

That's why I'm trying to dream up something new
"Catch your dreams, before they slip away"
I caught most, if not all, long before today
Perhaps the dreams of my youth
just grew long in the tooth

Today they're all long gone and it almost seems
as if I may have chased the wrong dreams,
but I'm still trying to dream up something new
so that I'll always have at least a goal to pursue

I've been hoping for laughter ever after
as long as the joke's not on me (again)
If the entire concept turns out to be wrong
I guess that I'll probably still laugh along

At least my dreams all came true
before they got bent,
but these days I wonder where the hell they all went

Still in all I've been blessed with the life that I've led
and I'm enjoying what's left
since I ain't yet quite dead

and I'm still looking for "laughter ever after",
but that project isn't quite completed (yet)
By definition it's an on-going program
and of course you always get what you get

Sometimes what you get is not what you want
sometimes I'm not even sure what that is
I've asked myself that question so often
sometimes life seems more like a quiz

but fortunately, laughter is everywhere,
it's not difficult to find
that's why I always laugh with others,
not at them, because that's my favorite kind

A positive outlook affects what you see
at least that's the way things have worked for me
                Try to look at the light side
                (you can't see in the dark)
and life should resemble a walk in the park

Just keep in mind that people have been mugged
in that park, so keep an eye on where you're
walking and try not to get too distracted
by all that stuff going on up inside your head instead

Travel Lightly

I've listened to his words for years,
his musical arrangements a gift to the ears
with screaming gypsy violins
lyrics explaining away our original sins

Flames engulfing Joan of Arc,
Reeling through the lilac park
well into his 80's and still an international star
(he used to play one mean guitar)

Leonard Cohen recently passed away
and his work continues to impact
many of us who still write today

But as I listened to his final CD
"You Want It Darker?" the day before
Thanksgiving, or perhaps that night,

as I listened to his song "Traveling Light".
I realized with horror, that's the title of the song
I had been writing that week!" (before hearing his)

So, I knew I had to change the title of my song,
and I modified it as I wrote along, instead of
calling mine "Traveling Light", I changed it slightly
                    to "Travel Lightly"

because it is partially about learning how to travel
lightly which of course is essential if you travel by
motorcycle as I often do, especially if there are two
of you riding in tandem to enjoy the view

It's also about everything else I have or haven't
learned from all the women I've known over the
several decades and especially one who has
passed away because she is still shining light
on the path I travel today, a path I

Travel Lightly

There was a time, now long ago,
when you and I were as one, you know
you rode with me, we followed the sun
back in those days when we were as one

we traveled light until the end of days
then into the darkness during the final phase
Burning deep into the night
we continue on our separate ways

and it never ceases to amaze how lightly
we traveled back in those days
When you travel light, there's not much heat
running cooler on the street

Rolling quickly down the road
traveling light without a heavy load
There's not much there to hold you back
traveling light and right on track

There's nothing left to leave behind
We traveled light to see what we could find,
and those memories still travel lightly
through my mind

Travel Light, just follow the rays
that lead you on until the end of days
when the light will fade from view
as the night descends on you

There will be no more light from the sun,
just light from the stars, scattered throughout
a night I once thought of as ours
Then came a day the light left your eyes,
and it took me a while to realize

You were just returning
your light to the skies
I hadn't yet seen
through our disguise

We were both made from the dust of a
collapsing star, Traveling Light is all we are,
There really is no end of days
just transformations along our ways

There was no beginning
There will be No End
Travel Lightly
My Old Friend

Penned on Black Friday, 2016
Thank You Betty (and Leonard Too!)
and while we're at it, thanks to all of You
for listening all the way through
as I've tried to share my thoughts with you
and may you all Travel Lightly too!

Rounding the Final Turn

I'm still a part of the human race,
but these days you won't find my face
at the starting line because I've found
another place that seems to fit just fine

I'm no longer at the beginning,
certainly closer to the end, but as
I've moved from place to place,
Here and there I've found a friend

Yet many seem to have drifted off
and some have, passed away,
but I find (much to my surprise)
that I'm still here today

With words still left unsaid
along the way, that has twisted
through the years to place me here
where I intend to stay

As long as I am able, although now I know
everything is temporary
especially you and me
(something that has taken quite a while to see)

I feel as if I'm rounding the final turn,
and I still have energy left to burn
in fact today I'm feeling fine
and can't even yet see the finish line

More Short Stuff

Part Time Memories
Dream On
Trail Markers
Not Lumbering Anymore
Different Faces
Good Morning
High School Sweet Hearts
Trackless Wastes
Not Much Improvement (Yet)
No More Gold Left in the Mine
Another Senior Moment
Echoes
The Alchemist
Just Beyond Our Reach
What's Your Hurry?
Rattle and Bang
Cliché
Only the Rocks Remain
Time Out
No History Made Here Today
A Page From the Dharma Diary
Satellite Junky
Guess That I Guessed Wrong
Fresh Ingredients
Patiently Waiting
You're Probably Used to That
If I Can Make it to Midnight

Part Time Memories

Sometimes I remember all of the things
I drink and take drugs to forget

I guess I really haven't
quite forgotten them yet

By now I realize there is no such thing as never and
accept that I may recall some things over and over

forever, but I'll keep trying for as long as it takes
not to keep repeating the same mistakes

and that may take quite a while because
repeating mistakes has always been my style

Dream On

All of your planning
and all of your schemes
may not match this world up
with the ones in your dreams

Trail Markers

I realized several years ago that my
writings and photographs are an attempt

to leave a record of what I've done
in an effort to figure out what we are
and to leave a sign as a mark
along the path I travel today

that may aid some other traveler
to find their own way

along a similar path
trod on some long distant day

Not Lumbering Anymore

The fence by the Lumberyard had been there
for years with a painted caricature of a handyman
running with a board under his arm:
>"Rapid Ralph" was their trademark

Then one day Ralph was apparently overcome
by his zeal when some graffiti artist closed a loop
below the letter "P", added some foam around
his mouth and he became "Rabid Ralph"

I really liked the change in his Personality

Different Faces

We've all worn different faces in different places
lived in different times and spaces
in the here and now we run wild and free
Someday the future will be a memory

We don't remember everything
There's a lot that we forget
and there's no way of knowing
what hasn't happened yet

Just do your best to be aware
of how we get between here and there
Try to remember where you are
balanced between an atom and a star

Good Morning

Shrugging off
a sleepy yawn
eager faces
greet the dawn

Darkness fades as day begins
Happy smiles and tired grins
Here and there a frown or two
at thoughts of things we have to do

High School Sweet Hearts

Stolen kisses
awkward gropes
fervent wishes
unlikely hopes

Burned once again
by the searing fire
of unbridled lust
and untamed desire

Trackless Wastes

The pages are not numbered
or indexed in any way
so I rarely re-encounter
what was written yesterday

169

Not Much Improvement (Yet)

Despite having hoped
for a better tomorrow
I woke up this morning
to today which is exactly
how my day went yesterday

Not Much Improvement (Yet)

No More Gold Left in the Mine

There is no more gold left in the mine
although there was at one time

Now only bats fly to and fro
They have nowhere else to go

Another Senior Moment

About half way through the performance
my mind just went blank

and that happens a lot
I'd call it another "Senior Moment",

but I just forgot
(Did I mention that happens a lot?)

Echoes

The road was too rough to ride on
so we got off to walk
and we walked on in silence
in dust too thick for talk

There's not much to speak of
between us although I tried anyway,
but the silence speaks volumes
and echoes in the quiet of the day

The Alchemist

He spent his life with a lump of lead
trying to turn it into gold, he said

No, the lead never turned into gold,
and since the alchemist is long dead

his body has turned
into mold instead

But then the lead turned
into something else too

It glisten's in the dark of the lab
as the body of the alchemist

molders on the slab
with no use or need for gold

Just Beyond Our Reach

We reached for the Stars
but settled for the Moon
because you can't
walk on the Sun

What's Your Hurry?

I have no need for a starting gun
faster than a bullet is not the way I run
in fact I'd rather not run at all,
and I'll never be at your beck and call

I'd rather just stroll down the boulevard
running there is much too hard,
so you won't find me at the starting line
rambling along suits me just fine

Rattle and Bang

The beat is what matters
not the words they sing
cast like stones from David's sling
it's that rocking, rollicking rattle and bang
bouncing off your ears like the songs they sang
not meant to be read but sung aloud
by the uplifted   voices of the crowd
with a rhythm that rises up from the street
        all that matters is the beat

Cliché

Of course, that's a cliché, but using them is OK
they can describe what you are trying to say
(I'm pretty sure they were designed that way)

Only the Rocks Remain

The Ancient Ones are gone now
Only the Rocks Remain
and even they have changed a bit
now weathered by wind and rain

Only traces of the places
where families shared their meals
remain in front of the holes and caves
that show us how it feels

to emerge from the earth each
morning as the sun rose over the rim
to draw water from the river in the canyon
and perhaps pause for a swim

Water carried to nurture corn, beans and
squash to feed children of the earth
who were born and lived then traveled on
leaving pictures on rocks, a hidden surprise

to show us the earth through their eyes
Pictures we can find today although
their makers have long passed away

Pictures of animals that were hunted
to provide meat that would sustain
the Ancient Ones who came before us
where Only the Rocks Remain

Time Out

Time is precious so they say
so make the most of each and every day
Time is like a river that only flows one way
We are all flowing downstream

Sometimes awake sometimes in a dream
flowing eventually to the sea
where individual time-streams
flow together and blend

into an ocean of time
deeper than a well
although I can't say when
           only time will tell

No History Made Here Today

We are not here to make or repeat history
we are here to live day by day
to continue that portion of history
we were born into as we travel on our way

mindful of those who came before us
and the world only our children will know
after we have traveled on to wherever we may go
        "Time Has No Boundaries for Us"

A Page From the Dharma Diary

My Karma stopped at the corner, and I stepped out
into a new life unlike the ones I had known before
taking my place somewhere in between
at least they told me I was there, although

don't remember: It started out in January,
and lasted through December
Another Spiral around a Sun
that ended as it had begun

The ending of another Year,
begins another one I fear
Actually it's not the beginning
or the ending: It's what comes in between,

Especially all those little parts
that we have not yet seen
I don't fear the future,
but I can't relive the past

I find myself stuck in between,
that's all that seems to last
here and now or now and then
repeating over and over again

spinning on a planet
spiraling around a star
we go through life from day to day,
and I'm still not sure exactly what we are

Satellite Junky

Turned into an electronic junky after
they wired me to a satellite dish
and once they had the hook set
just reeled me in like a fish

There are dozens of TV channels
plus the world wide inter web
They get you coming and going (that's twice)
so regardless of which way you're headed

you're going to have to pay the price
if you want to continue to receive the signal
on your particular device, which you will
once you become a satellite junky

and if you have a personal computer,
cell phone or TV you too may already be
a satellite junky just like me

Guess That I Guessed Wrong

I always thought that it was meant to be,
but it wasn't sometimes the magic works
and sometimes it doesn't

Fresh Ingredients

All of our families were immigrants,
except for those who got here first,
and those Native Americans have been
demoted to second class citizens
and that's not even the worst.

Some of the earliest immigrants were
kidnapped and dragged here against their will,
and you don't have to look very far to find some
who consider them ancestors living here still.

My own grandparents came from
Glasgow, Scotland so my dad was the first
Generation Born in the USA, and if this county hadn't
let his parents in, I wouldn't be here today.

It doesn't make much sense to keep people out,
although they should probably pledge their obedience,
because if you want to maintain a healthy diet
you have to use fresh ingredients

Patiently Waiting

None of the ancient pottery
bowls, cups and vases buried
in sands that cover all traces
of the people who used them
                          are lost

They are just patiently waiting
for us to stumble upon them
to realize that we are very similar
to their long vanished makers

You're Probably Used to That

Although it still feels as if I'm winning
I realize I'm merely nearly closer to the
ending than I am to the beginning

Ask people who have a lot of stuff
and most of them will tell you,
"Too much is never enough!"

The trick is to be content
with exactly what you've got
even if that is not a lot

That way you'll always feel OK
at least throughout most
of each and every day

Happiness isn't based on things
It's based on the joy
that each day brings

So smile to keep your life on track
and you'll discover
folks will smile back

you may also discover
that you are still flat broke,
but you are probably
already used to that

(I know I am!)

If I Can Make It To Midnight...

That's just a skeleton on my back,
the monkey is back in closet (for now),
but I live in fear of the day it might
step back out and climb back on

Doesn't matter what I may say
                    sooner or later
I'll misbehave in some way
I haven't done that (yet) today
If I can make it to midnight,
                    I just might be OK

Tomorrow never gets here anyway
so I'll Just concentrate on today
If I can make it to midnight
I should be OK

                    (What time is it anyway?)

Doesn't matter, ya'll ride
with your eyes wide open
on your way home tonight

Try to keep the shiny side
of your ride up
and the rubber side down,

but most of all ENJOY THE RIDE!

                    Because We Ain't Dead (Yet!)

Colophon

Brought to you by Wider Perspectives Publishing, care of James Wilson, with the mission of advancing the poetry and creative community of Hampton Roads, Virginia. This page used to have many cute and poetic expressions, but the sheer number of quality artists deserving mention has superseded the need to art. This has become some serious business; please check out how *They art...*

Travis Hailes- Virgo, thePoet
Nick Marickovich
Grey Hues
Madeline Garcia
Chichi Iwuorie
Symay Rhodes
Tanya Cunningham-Jones
          (Scientific Eve)
Terra Leigh
Raymond M. Simmons
Samantha Borders-Shoemaker
Taz Weysweete'
Jade Leonard
Darean Polk
Bobby K.
          (The Poor Man's Poet)
J. Scott Wilson (TEECH!)
Charles Wilson
Gloria Darlene Mann
Neil Spirtas
Jorge Mendez & JT Williams
Sarah Eileen Williams
Stephanie Diana (Noftz)
Shanya – Lady S.
Jason Brown (Drk Mtr)
Ken Sutton
Crickyt J. Expression

Se'Mon-Michelle Rosser
Lisa M. Kendrick
Cassandra IsFree
Nich (Nicholis Williams)
Samantha Geovjian Clarke
Natalie Morison-Uzzle
Gus Woodward II
Patsy Bickerstaff
Edith Blake
Jack Cassada
Dezz
M. Antoinette Adams
Catherine TL Hodges
Kent Knowlton
Linda Spence-Howard
Tony Broadway
Zach Crowe
Mark Willoughby
Martina Champion
... and others to come soon.

the Hampton Roads Artistic Collective (757 Perspectives) & The Poet's Domain are all WPP literary journals in cooperation with Scientific Eve or Live Wire Press

Check for those artists on FaceBook, Instagram, the Virginia Poetry Online channel on YouTube, and other social media.
Hampton Roads Artistic Collective is an extension of WPP which strives to simultaneously support worthy causes in Hampton Roads and the local creative artists.

Made in the USA
Columbia, SC
21 January 2023